Multiplying the Moon

Page from the 1901 census with details of the occupants of 87 Nelson Street

Myra Schneider

Multiplying
the Moon

*For dear Joe
with much love
Myra
December
23
2004*

ENITHARMON PRESS

First published in 2004
by the Enitharmon Press
26B Caversham Road
London NW5 2DU

www.enitharmon.co.uk

Distributed in the UK by
Central Books
99 Wallis Road
London E9 5LN

Distributed in the USA and Canada
by Dufour Editions Inc.
PO Box 7, Chester Springs
PA 19425, USA

ISBN 1 904634 04 4

Enitharmon Press gratefully acknowledges the
financial support of Arts Council England, London.

British Library Cataloguing-in-Publication Data.
A catalogue record for this book is available
from the British Library.

Typeset in Bembo by Servis Filmsetting Ltd, Manchester
and printed in England by
Antony Rowe Ltd.

ACKNOWLEDGEMENTS

Poems in this collection have appeared in:

Acumen, Aireings, Ambit Equinox, European Judaism, Foolscap, In The Company of Poets, an anthology of poetry by writers connected with the Torriano Meeting House, edited by John Rety (Hearing Eye Press 2003), *Interpreter's House, The Inquirer, The London Magazine, Magma, Making Worlds,* an anthology of poetry by contemporary women poets edited by Gladys Mary Coles, Dilys Wood and Myra Schneider (Headland Press 2003), *The North, Orbis, Other Poetry, Poetry London, Prop, Quadrant* (Australia), *Quattrocento, The Reader, The Rialto, Scintilla, Seam, Second Light Newsletter, Writing My Way Through Cancer* (Jessica Kingsley 2003).

'Voicebox' won first prize in the Scintilla Poetry Competition 2000.

I would like to thank the following people:

Erwin Schneider, who continues to accept that I am a compulsive writer and to give me an enormous amount of practical and emotional support, also for his unstinting help and support during the time I was ill in 2000; John Killick, who for twenty years has given me feedback I trust on everything I've written; Caroline Price for her perceptive and in-depth comments on my poems; Mimi Khalvati for her rigorous, insightful and generous criticism; the N7 workshop for thoughtful feedback; Stephen Stuart-Smith, my poetry publisher since 1994, for believing in my work and for all his support and consideration.

CONTENTS

Snowdrops

As I stare at the small
white heads, their circular bed
set in a bald frontage,
the afternoon swells
with distress. I imagine picking,
imagine pressing layers
of green-rimmed petals
to my chest to cover
the emptiness which will shout
when I lose my left breast.

Though they look weak
beneath a bush's crude
black spread of branches
these are not drops, crystals,
bells that ring thinly,
not hangdog ninnies,
timid girls running out of breath.

They have heaved through
weighty clay lumps,
speared freezing air
to bloom without summer's prop –
are more daring
than can-can poppies,
fiercer than the swimming
open-mouthed fear that wants
to devour me. They stand
uncowed by the north wind,
its sudden bluster, cruel bite.
And as I move on, each flower
fills me like an annunciation.

Today There Is Time

to touch the silken stillness
of myself, map its landscape,
the missing left breast, to lay
my nervous palm softly
as a bird's wing across
the new plain, allow
tears to fall yet rejoice
the surgeon has scraped
away the cancer cells.

Today there is time
to contemplate the way life
opens, clams, parts, savour
its remembered rosemaries,
spreading purples, tight
white edges of hope, to travel
the meanings of repair, tug
words that open parachutes.

Bath

Kindness, an Irish lilt in her voice,
spares me the effort of running the water
and supports my elbow when, stripped
of everything but wound dressings,
I take a giant step into the tub.

Warm water wells into my crotch,
unlocks spine, lullabies stomach.
Is it because I've passed through
such extremity this comfort is intense
as the yellow that daffodils trumpet?

Yesterday – my raw body stranded
by the basin, chill sprouting on my skin
while a Chinese student nurse
conscientiously dabbed each
helpless area – is miles away.

Dimly, I remember a stark room
and the high-sided saltwater bath
I was dipped in a few days
after giving birth. As Kindness
babies my back with a pink flannel

I'm reborn though maimed, ageing.
And this pool of bliss can no more
be explained than the song that pours
from a lark as it disappears into
stitchless blue, the seed circles

that cram a sunflower's calyx,
day splashing crimsons
and apricot golds across the sky
before it seeps into the silence
of night, the way love fountains.

The Cave

Rocks wall me in. Their turbulent layers
jammed together press unbearably
on my head. The clammy air spawns
moisture beads on ledges, ridges,
trickles down long stone faces.
Feeble light and the passages ahead
offer a darkness more profound
than anything I've ever known, imagined.

Stalagmites reach from floor to roof,
a mean band of skeletons waiting
to embrace me. An owl call becomes
a human voice lengthened as if
it had travelled down a pipe: the father
I thought I'd escaped. His hollow sentences
swell, resound on the cave walls:
'It's your own fault you're so fallen –

if you'd stayed in your inconspicuous place
you'd not be wombless now, not be one-
breasted, hardly a woman.' The words
rush at me: huge-winged birds
greedy to tear and gobble. Nowhere
to retreat. In a moment my sad flesh
will be stabbed, my bones broken.
But a small *no* begins to form

in my head. It holds the inimitable blues
of the Mediterranean Sea and I manage
to cry: 'I've become a deeper me.' Slowly
I back from the final judgement, body
flat to the rockside. At last I spy
the eye of day, am spewed onto a hillside,
feel the rough sweetness of bell heather,
the bright sky beginning to heal me.

The Shell

is smooth as a white mushroom cap,
conical, married to the rifts and curves
of a hill's sienna flank, and its spiral
soon culminates in a satisfying nipple.

Shall I scoop up this shell, go
down to the field where no sheep
graze, plant it on the forlorn flesh,
pretend my chest's refound its shape?

Better to recognize the protuberance
is large as an igloo, hug the side
to soothe my wound, its flood tide
of anger redder than rosebuds,

than the mountain's pelt or my blood.
Once I've found a way inside
I'll ignore the mother-of-pearl wall,
hurry down the corridor, climb all

the stairs, break the silken silence
as I bore a hole in the roof, untie
my coiled rage, let it erupt,
fan into flames that sweep the sky.

Elsewhere

How to approach this territory?
The slopes are beautifully sculpted
but are they based on rock layers
or a vacuum which will suck me in?
Even if the magnolia surface can bear
my weight I've no reason to suppose
I can remain queen of my legs.

There is no choice. Terrified,
I start to climb, know at once
potent invaders have forced entry,
are racing through my blood, taking over.
Unnerved, my body wavers, begins
to fight back. What resources
can I muster to contain the battle?

Somehow I must manage the ascent
to the crest with its crown of gold
and lemon crescents which could be
poised tongues, then pass through
the opening within the ring of peaks
and move beyond elsewhere to meet
snow-white clouds banked with possibility.

AMAZON

for Grevel

For four months
all those Matisse and Picasso women
draped against
plants, balconies, Mediterranean sea, skies
have taunted me
with the beautiful globes of their breasts as I've filled

my emptiness
with pages of scrawl, with fecund May, its floods
of green, its irrepressible
wedding-lace white, buttercup gold,
but failed to cover
the image of myself as a misshapen clown

until you reminded me
that in Greek myth the most revered women
were the single-breasted
Amazons who mastered javelins and bows, rode
horses into battle,
whose fierce queens were renowned for their femininity.

Then recognizing the fields I'd fought my way across
I raised my shield
of glistening words, saw it echoed the sun.

LAVENDER

for Angie

With a sachet of lavender secreted inside it
the purple bag is plump as a small bird's
breast, echoes your voice, its restful
clarity. When I slide my thumb down
the velvet underside a sense of psalm

fills me and dark cat night sidling in,
fitting the mound of herself to
a human back. I picture tension easing
in the day-to-day shifts we make
with those we're knitted to. Though I'm weak

the emperor-purple gloves my skin
awake, rallies the brain's metropolis, sends
pungent messages to the pulsing townships.
For months my braced body's fought
the indiscriminate battalions sent in to rout

any cancerous cell filching a plot
of land but now it's flagging, wants
to hunch in a ditch, weep at its wounds.
Useless to wish frailty was a boiler suit
I could unbutton – it's married to the roots

of my hair, my blood. But this pouch
you chose for me, its insistent coolth,
raises a garden where flowering bushes
are blue-leaved and threaded with bee thrum,
raspberries spill ripeness on my thumbs.

When It's All Over

I'm going to throw open my windows and yell: 'halleluiah',
dial up friends in the middle of the night to give them
the glad tidings, e-mail New South Wales and Pacific Palisades,
glorify the kitchen by making sixteen summer puddings,
watch blackberry purple soak slowly into
the bread and triumph over the curved glass of the bowls.

When it's all over I'll feed my cracked skin
with lavender and aloe vera, lower my exhausted body into
foaming suds scented with honey and let it wallow,
reward it with a medal, beautify it with garlands of thornless roses,
wrap it in sleep. Then from tents of blurred dreams
I'll leap like a kangaroo, spout like a whale.

Once it's over I'm going to command my computer to bellow
'Land of Hope and Glory,' loudspeaker my news
down these miles of orderly streets where the houses wear
mock Tudor beams and plastic Greek columns, dance
the Highland Fling in front of controlled tubs of cockerel geraniums,
sigh with enormous satisfaction when I make the evening headlines.

When it's finally over I'm going to gather these fantasies,
    fling them into my dented and long lost college trunk,
        dump it in the unused cellar
           climb back to strength
                up my rope of words.

PIANO

after La petite pianiste, robe bleue, fond rouge *by Matisse*

So enticing: her babyblue dress,
its wide collar, her marriage
to the piano that's dressed in a foxy red
and sienna body, the glide

of her hands over its white teeth.
So beguiling the open pages,
their notes fantasies that echo the wild
dance of bouquets across the gold-

edged arches on the coral wallpaper.
He's made her the focal point:
a skyblue body with damson clefts,
two held-out sticks that drift

into the keys and a craning neck stem
which blooms into a pasty blob
capped by brown, notched with a bead
eye. He's not interested in the seed

hidden at her core. If she's longing
to become someone she must
unstiffen those gawky arms, muster
her rounded shoulders, fluster

the ferny pot plant, her meekly
tucked hair, the pages
of scored music and, throwing a stone
at the piano, compose her own.

CARPET

after Red Interior, Still Life on a Blue Table *by Matisse*

Forget milky, silky, cool –
    I can't breathe without colour. Today I've dyed
my hair farmyard yellow and by squandering
    carmine, scarlet and vermilion all over my palette

I've concocted a shade that topples
    gloom, papers the walls, carpets the floor. Ignore
my black as liquorice thoughts, the way
    they zig-zag the room – wild horses won't stop them!

Only the Mediterranean table
    defies redness. The plate undulating on its surface
is an iced lagoon but the random apples
    are such a tempting crimson it crosses my mind

they've been poisoned. No, I won't
    throw them out. Risk is irresistible as diamonds.
Who wants the lined box of safety?
    Turn up the Beethoven and I'll bite the white flesh.

When I open the French windows
    red gallops onto the balcony, tries to swallow
deckchair stripes, fins of palms,
    then sprawls over the hot roofs by the shore.

But the bay's triumphant blue
    sweeps on, absorbing everything. It makes me
itch to stop the riot in my carpet,
    roll it up, fling my parcelled self into water.

DANCER

after La Danseuse créole *by Matisse*

Her tough stem is unstoppable,
grows from geranium and hot
cinnamon ground, has a charisma
that Jack's beanstalk lacks.

The jaunty green triangle
that's her belly comes acutely
to the point at her solar plexus.
She's not still for a moment –

branches into a spiky leafery
of arms and legs to offer
acrobatics laced with laughter.
Expect chillies at her finger-ends.

A marguerite frills over the fuss
of her breast. When she opens
the mouth in her velour seedbox head
it's full of the sky's blue fruit.

Once you tap into her body's twirl
pain will unknuckle, grief flake off
like old skin and, snapping fingers
at death, you'll calypso out of darkness.

CHOOSING YELLOW

for Les

Because I've insisted on yellow you write saying
porsche yellow's your favourite, define it as the buttercup
of Hohenzollern blended with Habsburg's rich
egg yolk, want to know which shade I prefer.
Immediately I see
        my child self plunging
hands into dandelion ranks bugling brightness
from a dirt pavement, see my paint-brush laden
with liquid gold from a cube, filling outlines
of fairytale caskets
        see the petals we sold as butter
on the paint-needy bench by the barbed
wire field opposite our house while far below
the great grey slugs of warships sat motionless
on the Clyde's highway.
        An echo of that colour
on my kitchen cupboards which like the past
are always clicking open. It's stronger
than the lemon
        I've seen infiltrating hard
green fruits in Andalusian orchards, quieter
than the skin of the plump lemon that's sitting
in my larder. When I cut slices the zest
stings my nicked finger,
        resurrects the curtains
with uneven hems I made years ago
to keep the kitchen from heat's stare, from cold
feathery with frost. Winter pecking at flesh
summons up

that unyielding oilskin with a hood
my mother made me wear whenever it rained,
not knowing I was torn to ribbons on the school bus
by the hot pack chanting: *yellow chicken*.
The shameful label, still stitched to my body,
jumps me to a badge
                    I've only seen in black
and white photographs: the star Hitler forced
other Jews to wear . . .
                    Yellow is the percussion
of light beneath clouds heavy as persecution,
the sweetness running from waxy cells, the body
soft as fur when pain's sharp gold embroidery
is unpicked.
        It sings from the bumblebee slash
on a motorway truck, wild flowers massed
on grass: celandine, lady's slipper, tormentil,
tiny warriors pitting themselves against
air fogged with chemicals . . .
                        You see I can't extract
a single yellow. It's a bittersweet colour
which feeds emptiness in the middle of the night,
a state of mind that refuses fear. It's any place:
thistle field, ditch, shore with shifting sand
where hope survives.

THE CAR

Unwanted as an elderly employee who's slowed down,
the car's been bumped over the brook in the park, stripped
of identity on the gravel under the viaduct

and abandoned by an owner who couldn't care less
that he's torn willow leaves, calm,
in his itch to turn the key in a faster model.

Every day I see how irresistible helplessness is,
wince at the wrenched wheel lying
like a lost foot. Nearby, spattered with dust,

the lopsided body peers through a ragged hole
and from the ground a hail of glass protests sharply.
Soon the felt carpet is rucked and fuzzed

as if by a factory of mice. I wonder if a fisted hand
walloped the back of the plastic baby chair
until it broke, if it was satisfying to knife the upholstery,

chuck condoms from the passenger window.
One sultry day I find the car burnt to death, its sides
unfleshed, the seats skeletal juts, the last shreds

of dignity snatched from the steering wheel,
the crown of the head rubbed gold
with rust. The air is still acrid with the smut of words

and I can smell the hot desire to destroy,
see how it ballooned as orange tongues licked
with fervour until fire gripped the mute frame. The murder

roaring in my ears threatens to swallow the energy
that cooks a meal, offers kindness, plans a bridge,
begins processes in the quiet of a womb, egg, cocoon,

which culminate in the black butterfly I've just seen
in the copse with red squares across its wings,
the rook on this tar-stained path, its beak tugging

at a paper bag full of bread, myself unravelling thoughts,
and the *must* insistent as the heart's pump, as breath
that pushes us through pain, through loss.

FLOOD

Last night rain begged, badgered
to enter my room, share my sheets.
I heard it ramming itself into the hole
in the guttering, felt it sink the garden,
drown pale hundreds of spread
sycamore hands and I knew the stream
in the park had swollen to a busy tongue
greedy for grass. In the dark of my head

flowered that first environmentalist,
Noah, who rated the world's species
highly as family. I saw him cooped
with milk-heavy cows, the mustard heat
of lion, pestered by droves of fearful voices.
Butterflies speckled the wooden dimness
with yellow, bee humming rose from the ark's belly.

When blue squeezed between the clouds
the old man climbed to the third storey
where owl moons and pigeon beads
lit a windowless attic. He lifted down
a dove and, mobbed by anxious relatives,
sent it into a cauldron of light. At last he lay
on the new green world's solid body
under the looped cloth of a rainbow.

But rain still pecked at my panes
and at sleep's border I found myself in the ark
designed by today's saviour: a sealed capsule
sleek as a whale that stabled two
of every make of car and carried a notice:
No animals for hygenic reasons.
The immense plastic bubble rode on waters
that stilled the North Circular Road,
its goose-grey flyovers, fluorescent cities.

I awoke to sunlight, to seagulls swimming
on rippling glitter in the park's basin,
a willow tree sprawled across a path.
And though squirrels whisked down
damp trunks to claw at the pale gold
of leaves, though children waded in pools
littered with bright pieces of sky,

I couldn't wipe the end of my vision:
how nothing remained after the ebbing
but tree stubs, concrete posts,
a few wheel hubs, mute screens,
mobile phones stuck in a limbo of mud,
and how the world shrank to an over-used
tennis ball in the palm of my hand.

THE BEANSTALK AND JACK

In three hours: a sprightly stem
that's jointed like a stork's leg
thick as a birch's silver trunk
and confident as bamboo. Jack
giggles at leaves big
as pigs' ears: 'I knew it was special.'

'A special dud, same as you –
throwing away our cow for a seed
and a bag of miracle powder.' Peeved,
Mum kicks the stalk which replies
with a hollow growl. Toes stubbed,
she slams into the house but Jack

mixes up a spray, watches tendrils
slither like lizards and curl up,
lime tongues suck in drops
from the silver mist over the garden.
The smug plant grows in leaps,
humiliates the sunflowers' blaze.

Next morning leafery taps a window
and Jack shins up the stalk, passes
shiny yellow pods which, in his greed
to reach the top he ignores. Prodding
the sky's blue, he crows with delight.
The plant quivers as he disappears.

A thousand bean bunches are glinting
in the midday sun when the lad
hares back pursued by the giant
bellowing about bones and bread.
As Jack skelters to the ground
the plant enfolds him in cooling leaves,

seems to welcome the axe he grabs.
At the first lop it falls to the ground
and the man roaring above, rocks,
collapses like a pricked balloon. Jack
gasps at the multitudes of gold pods:
'These are longer than a cow's legs,'

and yells to Mum, 'we're made for ever!'
'So you're a clever boy, not a clown!'
she gloats. Oblivious, the pair
trample rotting lettuces and mounds
of lifeless ladybirds. On the stalk's stump
buds appear, explode into leaf.

REINCARNATION

You sip wine from a frosted seagreen glass,
admire the shape, ask if it's recycled,
complain we're always binning stuff that's past
its best. Last week your phone was expelled
for losing its voice. Today the ailing car
gave up with a bleat. Soon metallic arms
will hug it to bits among the legless chairs,
plastic bottle necks, abandoned prams
heaped in hopeless mountains of waste. Suppose
biros could be reborn, or brussel spouts,
or dormice, or humans. If you could rise
again as bone china, a brook, a parrot
in gaudy flight, would you choose one of these
or a self feathered with brand new flaws?

THE ANT AND THE GRASSHOPPER

Ant

Oh put a sock in it! The snitter-snatter
of all that wing-scraping you call singing
is driving me mad. Life isn't constant noise
but slotting into your allotted place
in the colony. Life is industry:
building a nest for the fertile queen, shunting
food, rearing eggs, continuing for ever.

Grasshopper

That's dragging out a measly existence.
Life is the green smell of grass, hopping
through plump seedheads, all the tunes
legs and wings make rubbing together,
the sound as it lifts to the sky's warm
blue body. But scuttling about
on six boring legs under lumps of earth,
what inkling would you have of that?

Ant

Yes, I'm down to earth, not a flighty hopper
in green frippery. If you spend the summer
screeching how are you going to cope in winter?
Your airy fairying will stop when you find
your cupboard empty as Mother Hubbard's.
But if you nag us with stories of cold
and hungry we'll tell you to dance a jig
in a white field till your legs burn and you drop.

Grasshopper

Better to die in tango or jive than toil
like you. While you're busying and battling
I'm turning silence into a music
of many colours. It's more than work to use
your body as an instrument, play yourself
into an ecstasy of notes. But to you
with your one-track brain this will all be Greek.

Ant

Crazy to pass smart-arse judgements
on brains if you don't have one. When your huff
and puff have blown away and you're stiff
as frozen grass I'll laugh myself silly.

Grasshopper

I've the wit to see you're riddled with jealousy.
We live in clover for our natural span,
don't fancy hanging on to suffer the slings
of winter. Besides, humans adore our songs,
put them on shining disks. After death
our voices rise in their summer glory.

Ant

Stay in cloud-cuckoo land, whistle yourself
into the great reaper's mouth but stop wasting
my time with your claptrap! I need to get back
to heave and hustle, warn and swarm –
the real buzz you'll never get from life.

THE MAGIC FLUTE

To begin with we stare into the huge nothingness
exposed by boards, flies, wings, wires.
Not even a feather floating in a shaft of light.

Grey figures appear and sit cross-legged
as if at a loose end. How to hold onto belief
that colour and voice will bloom in this place?

Sound shimmers in the darkness, a figure
in princely red strolls beneath silken clouds. Soon
he's falling in love with the portrait of a princess

and we are in love with the music, the enchantment
it threads. But what are those shadow sets
of shapes shifting restlessly on the backdrop?

We make out heads, shoulders, arms and it dawns:
we're watching our rustling selves. A spotlight
travelling the stalls chooses a girl in white.

Cloaked in our longing, she edges her way
to the aisle, crosses a bridge over the orchestra pit.
The moment hands crown her with ringlets

all of us shed the ordinary's tight skin,
follow the path into fairytale's wood, join
in the difficult search for truth. The flute's tune

protects flesh and breath from any harm
when we undergo trials of fire and water.
Our throats melt as song unites the lovers for ever.

But the heroine takes off her flaxen wig,
the hero folds away his velvet jacket.
Hand in hand they cross the bridge, turn back

into us trailing inadequate selves, clutching
at seedpearls as we weep for wrinkles,
wreckages, the stage empty again.

Plums

Katie

– like an oasis in this desert of house,
plump yellows winking at me from the flat-
bottomed bowl, their skins cool as pottery.

Touch them and I forget I'm limp and lumpy,
fit partner for this mangy sofa, forget
this boring semi.   I suppose I stay here to pretend
I'm still Katie who married, had children
rose to the dizzy heights of head of English,
as if I'd not awakened numb, a nothing
washed up beyond the middle of my life.

These gorgeous plums make me picture
fat pillows, arms giving, hands cupping.
And I love the painted lemons, the easy leaves
that roam across the dish to a rim blue
as the sea far below Taormina
                    – oh that town
bolted to jags of rock, its zig-zagging alleys,
steep steps, shops jammed with joyful bowls.

But Frank was fixated on Etna:
'We're a stone's throw from a marvel
of a mountain but you want to drool over tat!'
Smarting, I didn't answer but refused
to rise at five, ride in an elderly coach.

Free, I pottered among carnivals of plates,
then clambered up above the pink roofs
until the Greek theatre was a toy, sat

on a terrace sipping iced coffee, sniffing
at wild thyme
                    and staring at Etna rising
above the bay, a giant with white shoulders
and head in clouds of smoke thick
as anger that's forced its way up and out.

But I didn't look at the rift between Frank
and me . . . Now I wouldn't want him back
even if he kissed good-bye to Australia
which he won't – he's snug in his newfound land.

It wasn't hard to paper over his absence
until I ripped the timetable from my life.
Oh stop moping!
                    Fling open a window
but don't run a finger down a pane
and tut because it's black as the cat.
Breathe in white hyacinths, new grass,
spot Dusky, her eyes trained on a bird.

Why's that lad across the road roaring
and rocking his wheelchair? He'll tip himself
onto the pavement and who'll be able to shift him?
Not his mum with those eyes that are hopeless
even when she smiles. His eyes glitter
with life, search faces, jab with demand.

For God's sake! she's flapping a teatowel –
she could be a scarecrow warning off
an enraged bull.
                    Get moving, Katie!
If only I had something better to distract him
than this plate of plums I'm cradling
as though it was a gift of golden eggs.

Quickwrite

William

Yack yack bummy Mum
fuss fuss fucky Mum
I'm not staying in this boaring room
just reeding about iceburrge seas
and monkees swinnging in tropicle trees
and writing on the computer.
I'm going to shoot my way out
yes jump into my racing car
drive faster faster down the moterway
take my mobile and my girlfrend
all sexy her cornfeeld hair.
From Heethrow I'll fly a plane
to Africa xplore its dark hart
and mistic mountins.
You can come if you don't talke to Mum
seen you befor
your blue door house.
Name WILLIAM I keep saying
Katy kitty catty Katey
purring at the pritty platey
Milly silly scummie mummy
yap yap yap yap.
Write you somthing
eezie peezie.

PLUM POEM

A plum is fun
A plum is the eggy sun gleaming
Im going to bite it
bang it wang it squawsh it to death.

When I swallow the sun
my skin will turn gold
and I'll be president
I'll be god.

Angel

Millie

Tea toffee-brown so a spoon
would stand up straight in it,
a bit of easy chair and a ciggy
now William's in bed and glued
to lions munching antelopes. Thank God
for telly. In a minute I'll watch dishy

Inspector Kellyrigg, forget everything.
Because of that performance outside
my head's killing me. I wish a flannel
was cooling it. Tantrums in the house
are one thing but he hasn't let off
such a box of fireworks in public

since he was small enough to pick up
by the scruff, jam into bed and lock
the sides. Now he's twenty-two
it's not a joke if he decides to throw
his weight about. I was in a pink panic
until *she* came flying across the road –

that angel with frizzy copper hair –
holding a bowl of plums, and wearing
a top with the kind of smocking
I'd try out if ever I had the time.
William was struck dumb by surprise
when she suddenly gripped his chair.

We've halloed across the street for years.
I watched her girls bike to the park,
grow up, fly the nest. Sandra
next door heard her husband had left –
men, what a shitty lot! Now she's stuck
in that swish house but she shines

with sympathy and listens – unlike
those know-alls from the council
yapping their heads off about everything
you can't have, offering stuff
you don't want, smirking at William
as if his brain was flea-sized.

Though she couldn't follow what he said
he took to her quick as a duck to water,
wrote jokes and a verse on his computer,
showed her the story he's just read,
and all his books on travel and climbing.
I could see she thought he was clever –

and she should know seeing she's a teacher.
When she offered to help him he trembled
like a jelly with excitement and a light came on
in my head: he could go to university,
be a poet. *Someone* up in the blue
has looked down and sent us an angel.

Library

Tom

Depressing to push the swing door
only to see racks of videos, cassettes,
slim disks, computers clicking
and winking, as if it's essential to draw

people in before exposing them to books.
The apple-green walls have been stolen
from an infants' cheerful classroom
and the plastic shelving on rollers looks –

is so lightweight. Books speak perfectly well
without girls in jungle-shrieking orange
but I suppose it's fusty to long for plain covers,
oak bookcases, off-white walls

incised by austere windows, to fear
we're moving into a brave new
bookless world whose printed words
only tremble on screens and disappear

the instant the delete button's pressed?
'Mr Shields – sorry to make you jump.
You asked for *Recent Roman Finds* – it's in.'
Nothing musty about Mrs West

with her rainbow skirt and striped tights,
her belief – though she must be close to retirement –
that the new technologies encourage reading.
God, that word keys in blank fright.

I have to decide in the next three weeks.
If I free myself to finish the history series
and turn to in-depth studies, I'll miss the kids,
even their truculence, be a permanent freak

sifting the past to escape the weight
and emptiness I carry from room to room
in my flat – that relentless mouth gabbling
self-pity, spitting words of hate . . .

There's Katie Marks, her auburn hair
wilder, face pale, translucent,
quite pre-Raphaelite. The staffroom's edgy
without her – she spreads a warmth that's rare.

'Tom, it's centuries since we had a chat
and before you ask about this zoo book
I'm planning to jump a disabled lad
into poetry with pictures of wild cats –

Tyger tyger burning bright
and Ted Hughes' jaguars. The boy
is half mad with boredom but has originality,
a feeling for words and he's full of fight . . .'

I hear myself saying: 'Why don't we meet
for a meal . . . Tuesday . . . The Eucalyptus Tree?'
My tongue's broken the rules and she's nodding,
cheeks red as tulips. I can't retreat.

Asparagus

The glass tables each with a single white
tulip in a tubular vase, the long bar
doubled by a glitzy wall mirror, tubs

with small eucalyptus trees, giant cacti,
the cool clientèle – all these have turned them
into strangers. Tom searches for suitable words,

regrets he didn't phone and plead illness.
Katie, watching the skinny waiters quick
as eels, wishes she could unzip, hop

from her shapelessness, hates her aged skirt
and velvet top, sneers at the flutters she'd felt –
of course he'd only wanted a staffroom chat,

not realized that without the school's web
of smell and noise it would be unnatural
to dissect the head's gaffes or Wheelie Brown

setting fire to a table. How little she knows
about this angular man who's holding himself
too stiffly. His face is kind but his eyes

are pale marbles and the lines across his brow
make her picture seals, their black wrinkles.
'Asparagus?' he suggests from behind the menu.

She wants to say: 'I hate the stuff!'
instead politely agrees: 'a treat!'
And the green stems turn into penises

which dance with the fiery pistil tips
of heliconias painted across the wall,
with slender fingers ending in purple nails,

with the absurd pepperpot long as her arm.
She hears Tom querying: 'Tigers . . . teaching . . .
boy?' extricates herself, dismisses her vision

as pathetically teenage, describes William
laughing and shouting not at photos
of a leopard prowling, a lion body tensed

at the point of pounce but at the line:
Over the cage floor the horizons come.
'He made me re-read the poem three times,

put it on tape so he could listen to it at night
and when I left he was writing about a beast
with tusks and humps that could outstrip a car.'

Tom nods and his eyes are soft as wax
under candle flame. The asparagus
arrives. She dips a stalk into melted butter,

for the first time tastes the succulence
and to her surprise vents her anger with Alice:
'She phones regularly – daughter keeping tabs,

wants me to be oh so sensible, says
William will turn into a burden, nags me
about teaching him for next to nothing, sounds

like her self-sufficient father – you probably know
he took off to Australia, half-suggesting
I could follow?' Gentle as a summer dove

Tom asks: 'And do you miss him?'
'Not much but sometimes at home I feel
like a dry vessel in an empty dwelling.'

'I was married happily for two years.'
Tom's composure cracks. He gulps, continues
in a rush: 'Then she began disappearing

for days, weeks, came home dishevelled, ill,
flew into a temper however tactfully
I asked if there was someone else. In the end

she clammed up, had a complete breakdown –
she's been a wrecked person ever since.
I go to see her in hospitals, awful hostels.

If she's not completely lost in herself
it's non-stop accusations but she was –
could still be a talented artist . . .'

Katie sees he can't go on. His pain
is so palpable she could scoop it up.
She longs to sympathize – touch his hand,

doesn't dare to tamper with the wall he's built
to shield himself. Tears threaten her eyes –
for him? something she's longed for, never known?

She shares his silence, when the plates are cleared
asks about his *Ways into History* series.
He slips into his school manner, entertains her

41

with an anecdote about a piece of research
he's done for *The Anglo-Saxons*. And through
stir-fried ginger chicken, through mango sorbet,

while he drives her home they chat books.
When they part he mentions meeting again,
his voice closed, his face sheer as ice.

Beast

William

Me waring shorts and trainerrs,
me faster than an Olimpik sprinnter
running through feelds of brite grassis
and spottied flowers were bees bumbel
to a streem liying silver as a sorde.
Me leeping the water like a rasehorse
everyone else far behind.
Me by a grate mouth in the mountinside.
And inside it unroleing the sea
Kitty-Katty-Katie with her meeow cat
and krates of words
Klaws and Crakkers Craks and Kraters
Purpuls that swim to never
Moons cold as cutlerie.
Me she's talking to me. What's she saying?
Now my beast is cuming out of the cave,
my eggsact beast
orange bars acros its back
spikie humps and tuskes
growing from savidge jaws.
Mum's yapping 'I do all the donkkey work
you appeer for a day and spoyle him.'
Shout her down Dad tye her tungue

don't be a cowady cowady kustard.
Beast why are you staring at me
with those spining cercles?
It was me who mayde you.
Dont throw your blue flammes
don't shok me with your electrik strypes
don't bern me to nuthing.
If I could pushe out the shout
that's stuke in my throte
I'd wake up.

Paperweight

Millie

. . . solid glass and it just missed
my cheek, could have cracked my jaw –
it was all his stupid father's fault.
He's only home at week-ends,
on Friday shambled in hours late
bleating about the train being delayed.

Gone ten, William started
to jabber about the pub, and Ken –
not a smatter of sense in spite of
hundreds of books packing his head –
said: 'Why not!' though he knows
we need to nudge the boy to bed

before it's late or night acts on him
like a shot of heroin. I mean
he hee-haws as if he was a donkey,
hauls himself round the house
with his long arms until his eyes bulge
and he punches banisters, moths, anything.

If he'd not been cheated of muscles
from the waist downwards I'm sure
he'd have been something in sport. Though
his legs are limp as pillows his shoulders
are powerful as mountains. Inside, I cry
when he watches Olympic runners.

Anyway, Ken started arguing
ten past ten didn't matter.
That did it! In a frenzy William
snatched the paperweight with bits
like breadcrumbs trapped in the glass,
and yelling words I won't repeat

hurled it blindly. And what did Ken do?
Nothing. Opened and shut his mouth
like a fish, then slunk out of the house
as he always does at the first whiff
of trouble. Left me to sort out William
who was on the carpet biting and kicking . . .

I didn't mean to flood you with tears
but you're the only one who understands.
Sometimes I feel I'm a fly struggling
not to slide down the greasy side
of a jar and when at last I reach
its neck all I can see above me

is the top screwed on for ever.
But you've not come to hear me moaning –
I must wash this disgusting floor.
You'll find William banging on his computer
unless he's outside the door gobbling up
my words and grinning from ear to ear.

Coral

Katie

. . . Barking next door just as I'm drifting –
I could wring that dog's wretched neck
much as I love her spotty paws on the fence.
Oh blessed quiet, they've shut her up. Fuck,
she's off again, racketing on like Alice:

'Anti-social, mother, seven rooms for you
and a cat . . . if you gave up lame ducks
and bits of tutoring, went to adult classes
you'd make new friends.' Bloody patronising –
or maybe I'm wearing disenchanted glasses.

I wish her sister wasn't far away in Tobago
researching underwater life. When I visited
we were always laughing and I fed my eyes
on tulip trees, egrets feeding beside
tethered cows, pelicans roosting, bays

where the Atlantic edged untrodden sands
with lace. And Clara rowed me to the reef,
pointed to minute shoals flicking through
fronds, globes, corals with eerie branches –
I won't sleep now. I know what I'll do:

plant the tomato seeds, forget Alice spiky
with comments: 'They'll fail or you'll have a glut
at a time they cost almost nothing.' No soul,
no longing for the mystery of a fleck that sprouts
a threadlike stem with two leaves, a whole

fernery that in three months splutters fruit.
Yes, a waste of time for a woman high and dry
on her own – higher and drier since that meal
with Tom Shields three weeks ago. If I
hadn't laid out my problems on the table,

if he hadn't let me look into the place
where he hides his feelings, if we'd not
been completely in tune for half an hour,
I'd simply see him as a colleague: a teacher
with a flair for taming kids, a writer with the power

to breathe life into the distant past, a man
who ducks behind his sense of humour. Stop
mewling, get yourself to the computer, wing
an e-mail to Clara who loves William's poems –
tell her how anxiety makes Millie cling

to what she knows. The lovely girl's even tuned in
to the different kids I'm tutoring, who's a likely
for Oxford, who's a problem. Shan't let out
a word about Tom – I need to forget him . . .
She's always asking so I'll get a cheap flight . . .

Dusky purring and I'm sinking in water clogged
with tyres and coral twists, bits of my brain.
Who broke them off? Don't let them crumble.
Must fist my way to the surface, struggle
to the beach, prise myself open again.

Face

Tom

The Romans were easy, a gift. So teasing
the scraps about the Anglo-Saxons.
If the five personified senses
staring from the Fuller brooch's roundels
could speak they'd tell us so much. This morning
in the British Museum they spellbound
the fifth form until I stopped mid-sentence
at the sight of red hair. The kids thought

I'd lost my marbles. When the head turned I saw
sad eyes and a web of wrinkles. Mustered
my wits, of course, while the kids made notes
but the intense focus was lost. Absurd
to be disturbed by chat and sympathy
over dinner with an ex-colleague.
My life must be confined to work
and doing what I can for Ella.

Yesterday it wasn't enough. Her room,
its walls bald as shaven heads, its view
of puny trees marooned on a lawn,
that smell of food and disinfected floors
which never kills the odour of unwashed
bodies, of stranded, inactive selves,
oppressed me so much I hardly tried
to make her comb the knots from her hair,

or come out for some air and a pub lunch
so it was my fault she froze up. Beyond
her dead-fish eyes I couldn't help seeing
Katie's luminous as she talked about
that disabled boy eager for poems,
then almost unbearably gentle
as she listened to me. And I suddenly
felt a frightening urge to get away –

stamped it out by showing her some pictures
of Anglo-Saxon clasps. Usually
Ella laps up pictorial details
about my writing. But my timing
was wrong. 'You prefer dead jewellery
to me, I wish I was dead,' she whimpered
and tore the cards, threw them in the bin.
I itched to hit her, caught a glimpse of something

inviting and blue as the sea, let it
go, propelled her outside to the car.
She was expressionless as a doll
all afternoon until back in her room
a big-bellied woman kicked the door
open, screeched: 'Come and crack some plates
with Dell, girl!' Then up she jumped, shouting:
'Yeah, smash and smash them on his smug head!'

The pair of them chilled me with mad peals
of laughter but when Dell went she shut down.
I stroked her bitten fingers, sad face,
couldn't coax her out of her box . . .
The phone so late – something's wrong. 'Ella?'
'Hi Tomikins, will you chauffeur me
to a gallery next week? I think I'll gorge
myself on the Fauves, buy fat tubes of red –

must go, Dell's howling for me – kiss, kiss . . .'
The five hours of attempts to soothe her
must have worked after all. She means
to start painting. If I can make her stick
at it this time surely she'll begin to
believe she has talent, then couldn't she
be weaned off the pills that dumb her down,
couldn't she . . . we – get a life together?

Park

The light is back, whole bathtubs of it,
pools, lagoons to wallow in for months
before it drains away and November walls us
in darkness – this passes through Katie's mind

while she stands at a pedestrian crossing
by William in his electric chair and they're dazzled
by winking wing mirrors, windscreens glittering
in the stream of traffic which comes reluctantly

to a stop. Millie had begun a string of calamities
with: 'Not a snip of road sense,' but William's alert
at each junction. When Katie nods he switches on
and they cross, pass through iron gates

into the park. 'Grah, grah!' he exults, steering
over grass and she has a vision of him unhooked
from his weighty contraption, whooping, galloping
down the slope to the distant running track,

circling it at dizzy speed. They head for the stream
where willows elbow and lean their pristine
green heads. By a waterfall he holds out
spread hands as if to catch the white rush,

peers at bubbles in water dark as earth
in a hard winter. At last he's sated, turns,
points at the trees, gabbles questions. She picks
a thin leaf. He strokes it, smells it, lays it

against his cheek and, throat knotting in the middle
of the word, keeps chanting: 'Wi-oh, wi-oh',
gingerly touches a ridged trunk. Katie
is caught up in his elation yet almost crying

with fury: the piddling shops down the road,
a day centre on Wednesdays, the odd visit
to the pub with his Dad – can't they see he's starved
of life? She pictures Millie, face drained,

slight shoulders tensing and her rage dies
as she runs after William who's swerving towards
a rabble of ducks. A woman whose sunglasses
half hide her mealy face is chiding her dogs,

three little yappers with popping eyes:
'You lot, do as you're told.' Nodding at a drake,
its emerald neck outstretched as it pursues a duck,
she throws out: 'Men, all the bloody same.

I suppose you know females without a mate
are tupped in the water by every he around,
sometimes drowned.' And not pausing for breath:
'That's a monster of a chair, don't drive it into

my pettikins.' Katie bridles but William's hooked,
savouring every word. Neatly cropped grass
gives way to stalks flecked with buttercup yellow.
'Wanna geh ow!' He strains across the belt

and she itches to unbuckle it, to let him crawl,
roll, lie in the meadow, knows she could slide him
to the ground, worried that once out he'd fight
to keep his freedom. As she wavers

she's surprised to see Tom striding down
the path, hears herself quaver. 'How are you?'
He clasps her arm, pulls his hand back
as though the spontaneity was an error. Hurriedly

she explains: 'This is William and what he wants
is to sit on the ground.' Taking in the thin legs,
heavy torso and the eyes, two creatures
glinting above a lopsided grin, the earnest man

soon works out how to support the boy,
lowers him to the bright ground. At once
he slips free, swivels in a single movement
to his knees and pulls a daisy, face blissful

as if he'd landed in the garden of paradise.
Turning to Katie Tom says: 'You look lovely
in that flowery jacket.' She stoops to hide
her reddening face, points at a minute green spider

and he crouches beside her, shows William
an empty snail shell. Together they examine
its spirals. She allows the idyll for a while,
tries to sweeten its end by telling William

they might see a special bird by the stream
but the sun slips from his face and he lets out
an earsplitting 'Nah', raises a fist. Tom
distracts him with a joke and when he laughs

deftly lifts him into his chair. Katie waves
her gratitude but Tom's frowning now,
maybe at the sun, and she hurries after the chair
as it bumps away at speed. At the stream

what luck! Below the gleaming fold of the fall,
below its white tails, standing stock-still
in the water on legs stark as hedge parsley
in September: a heron, its beak a readied knife.

Heron Poem

William

Heron stands on stik legs
in the swish and swerl.
Heron ignaws the sliks of waterfall
which gleem like jelly.
His neck is long and thin
as a sentral heating pipe.
A sturn black line runs down his head.
Heron is silent as an aynshunt statyou
but he rules this water
and its white gubbling mouthes.

Blakker than a blakk coat
blakker than dust
blakker than Mum's blakk looks
a rooke swings darklee down.
Heron hooks rooke with a wickked eye
flaps and stabbs.
And its batle batle with coars
and cacks and thrasshing wings
all the way up the hill.
Rooke droopes disapeers
never to fighte again.
Heron has won.
Clap the vicktor clap clap.

At middnight when the moon
berns whitely in the sky
William kreeps out to kiss his grilfrend
and heron snaps his beek at Mum
awders her to come to the park
calls all the other mothers
to cueue up behind her.
Mum argews trembulls trys to sneek away.
Heron bangs a wing in her face.
'Shut up or I'll bite out your tung
skatter it to the 4 winds.
Kneel downe you grumppie woman
mix your fingers with soft grassis
cuvver your face with wyllow leaves.'
Mum falls in a heap of terroar.
Immortle heron xecutes a dance.

Brains

Millie

Try it out!
You must of left your brains at work, Ken Peters.
I mean how could a year stuck
in an ugly building at the far end of Wales help William?
It's hoodwink to tell him he could learn to look after himself.
Cruel. Like kidding him his legs could carry him
up a mountain . . .

Meet new people.
You might as well stick him on a desert island.
Nobody'd have a clue what he was spouting
and with thirty others, each sporting a bunch of problems,
who'd bother to sit with him and find out like Katie does?

. . . Trained staff?
for what? Not to teach book learning.
The one thing going for him is his brains, you know that.
But they'd steamroller over his intelligence – I'd put money on it –
plonk him by a knee-high stove, tell him to empty a packet of soup
in a pan, then give him a tick for learning how to cook.
Katie across the road – she'll push him through exams.
If he goes away it should be to university . . .

Realistic!!
You're telling *me* who's left holding the baby every bloody day
to be realistic . . .

You're joking.
It's too fucking late for me to have a life of my own,
me who's got a brain the size of a green pea
and not an inch of experience at anything.
Sounds like you're fishing for an excuse to send him away.
Lucky he's out at the park again and not listening in . . .

Just leave it, will you.
He'd have as much chance there as a snowball in hell.
Trust you to forget we let him go away six years ago
when he finished school. And what happened?
Bullied – he was bullied day and night until we rescued him . . .

You visit
if you think it sounds so marvellous
but I don't want to hear another whisper about it
unless you've got chapter and verse.

Letter

Katie

That smell of unsmutched warmth
from the morning ground, pungent
as washing drying. Everything
clear and clean. Dusky
rolling in a pool of gold,
sunlight slithering on her fur.

Now she's snaking into the syringa
and it's smudging her into the darkness
beneath its leafery. Already
the bush is covered with buds
waiting to burst into whiteness.
On such a day as this

I long for childhood, dabbling
in sand by the cloudless sea –
the sea William's never
set foot in. Tom was brilliant
with the boy – I might find
the nerve to ask him to drive us . . .

No exam kid due for hours
so I can sit and soak up
the outside with tea, toast
and the post – but it's all bumph
unless *Mrs. K. Marks* in clumsy
green writing is a real letter.

No, *The Cat Society* – begging me
for money, I expect, like every
other charity in Britain.
Oh God! *Cats in your neighbourhood
are being killed . . . mutilated . . . signs
on the bodies of ritual slaughter.*

What kind of mind made up this?
*The act of an extreme sect
other Jews would condemn . . .*
it's *horrible* like pinning on the Jews
the death of a child in Lincoln
eight centuries ago.

The whole world is riddled
of compulsive haters – did one
underline my Jewish name,
know I had a . . . 'Dusky, come in,
milk!' . . . Irrational to lock doors
as if the sun's a prying eye.

This nastiness jumps me back
to school when I was eight,
the class turning on me, chanting
my name: 'Steinberg is a stinkberg,
a slimeberg!' It must have lasted
a few weeks but it felt like ever.

And now this hounding has landed
on my doormat. There's no end to it:

dictators, terrorists, countries always
at war, persecution for a skin colour,
a religion, a hump, a tic,
anything that labels you *different* . . .

I don't want this letter indoors
but burning it at the bottom
of the garden won't wipe
its words. I've got to steel myself
to fight it..confide in someone.
Not Alice – she'd subvert it

into a reason for moving. Clara?
Too distant to alarm and my closest
women friends have whizzed off
for half term. Tom? Suppose
I phone and if he's at home
ask for advice – low key . . .

'Tom, I've had a lunatic . . . stupid
to cry.' 'Katie, I'm coming round . . .'
Kettle on, clear the table –
and instead of this sick letter
keep playing to myself the lift
in his voice as he said my name.

Words

Tom

From the reclining chair in her garden
the world looked benign as a cushion,
its stillness undisturbed by the sun thinning
and fattening shadows, by her cat flicking
lazily at a fly, almost grinning,

or Raksha, a university hopeful, indoors
discussing Katie's comments on her essay.
Even my morass of Alfred notes
seemed more manageable away
from the untidy flat, its dust motes.

And suddenly I knew the focuses I wanted
for his early life. What made me stop
jotting points to yank a stone
from the rockery taken over by aubretia,
gawp at its clammy underside sown

with wriggling grubs and leggy insects?
It was as if I'd refused to let myself
forget for ten minutes how squirming,
devouring underpin the world of creatures
threaded with blood and that human worming

and preying is not a need for survival
but greed for power or hatred
stirred and fanned by fanatic minds . . .
The police sergeant who handled today's
piece of sickness was to the point and kind,

pronounced the letter a racist crime,
said thirteen others had been reported,
added: 'Not a whisper of missing cat
on this patch but keep yours in
for a while at night. Stroke her a lot,

you'll soon feel much better.'
I watched Katie's relief, the way
she unwound and after he took
the letter away it seemed natural:
coffee, chatting, sorting my notebook

while she gave an hour's lesson.
In the warmth I dropped off, woke

to see her at the kitchen door with a bowl
of glistening tomato slices and olives,
smiling: 'Will you fetch the rolls

from the table. And while we ate
she asked: 'What were you working on
today?' as if I was often around.
What prompted me to snipe at myself
for dozing off, then bound

into that silly fabrication of burning
the cakes – the only thing relating
to Alfred kids retain, and my intention
to excite them with his courage and skill
in battle before drawing attention

to his passion for books, his breadth of vision?
Katie, her eyes burning softly,
said: 'I was struck that he learnt to read
as an adult and afterwards wrote texts.
He must have understood the need

for literacy.' She nodded as I explained
this concept was unknown, that he hungered
for the learning and wisdom stored in books.
'Written language has such power
for good and evil,' she murmured and the look

on her face made me want to touch it.
How did we shift from Alfred's brilliance
to my wife? Was it Katie's voice, the play
of her hand on the cat's silky back
that lulled me into spilling the way

Ella periodically starts painting,
flowers into her genuine self,
then falls apart, gathers the stuff

of her anger to squirt at me before
she sinks into depression. 'Sounds tough,'

Katie frowned, then rattled me
by asking why I visited her so often
when she behaved with such hostility.
I pointed out we were still married.
'But is her life your responsibility?'

she insisted. Words flocked
into my head: I'd rather be here
with you – things I couldn't speak.
It was as if I was sitting beside Eve
in the garden of paradise and I was weak

with longing for sweet forbidden fruit.
'I could come with you when you next visit,'
she said, 'but I don't want to press
my company on you.' Why did I give in
to her offer, breath thumping, say: 'Yes'?

Sea Poem

William

I want this sea
this stewpendus neverending animul
that never sticks to one colur
and never setles down to sleep.

I want the waves
giant wariers leeping on the shore.
I want the white angery noyse in my head
and the hewge water draging
stones shells botles under
untile they droune.

I want the fome bubling
and cuvering my feet with cold
the gulls like mini airoplanes
flying the sky yeling at the sun.
I want to sit in a speedboat
betweene Katie and Tom
larfing as we swishe over xcited rowllers.

I want to knowsdive into the deep blue
be a sharke with poynted teeth
lye in wait until The Mother complayning
at the eddge of the water waydes in
then snapp her up.

The Ladder

Millie

. . . went behind my back, Katie,
how could he – Ken, I mean – sneak
William to the pub, fill his head
with pie-in-the-sky stories about *The Ladder*
yet not breathe one word to me
that he'd been to wildest Wales to see it.

He was fooled, of course by its gym, library,
field of sheep – and they've ganged up
like a pair of silly kids. Impossible,
William is now, treats me as if
I'm a wicked stepmother in a story.
Katie, you're the only person I can turn to . . .

A cup of tea would save my life –
I'm fit to drop . . . We *can't* send him
to that fancy place – I'd be sick with worry.
They don't believe in proper checking,

let kids in wheelchairs out on winding
country roads where cars could kill them.
And if parents complain they get uppity,
rabbit on about 'being real'.
So when a lout kicks someone
downstairs or the lonely cry themselves
to sleep they don't blink an eyelid . . .
I knew you'd see why I'm stewed up . . .

A little piece seeing as you made it . . .
Trying it out's a dead loss.
They're lovey-dovey with newcomers at first,
then drop them in the deep end.
Ladder, my foot, send him there
and he'd slide to the bottom rung.

There's only one answer: *you*.
William adores you. I want to pay you
to give him lessons more often,
visit more places. I know in my bones
you'd get him into a proper college . . .
It doesn't matter if it takes a long time . . .

Friends? He's never made friends
with disabled people, except once
with a puny thing who hero-worshipped him
for a year, then died. You're my only hope . . .
I knew you'd think about it, Katie,
I knew *you* wouldn't let me down.

Seaweed

Katie

If you fall off this shingle bank, William,
if this worked-up sea snatches and sieves you,
your mother won't forgive me. God, we're tumbling,

stones slithering in our wake. In seconds
we'll be five fathoms down – and our bones,
what will become of them? A stroke of luck –

the seaweed's breaking our fall but the green slime
and fleshy strands are unnerving as octopus limbs.
William, you're tangled in bladderwrack or is it afterbirth?

That paddling woman with a distorted face
and white legs is Millie. I'd make her listen to me
if she wasn't in a soundproof glass case . . .

At last, the rowing boat – I knew it would excite you.
My father used to take me out but he never
made it sing along, never turned the oars

into wings like Tom does. Once, I loved waves
but this black crest is going to capsize us.
I don't want to fall into these hopeless depths . . .

O-oh the water is shallow, clear as a bell.
Look at the mallow-pink fish swarming
through the coral heads. They're breaking up

just like Clara said. Soon none will be left.
There she is on the beach and she's waving.
Why's she shouting: 'Come and eat the sunset . . .'

Where's my lovely girl gone? Only sand bled
white and this palm tree propping up a ladder.
It's Tom at the top – how my heart gladdens.

He's taking off all his clothes, smiling at me.
'Please, Tom, I want you to lick the salt
from my wounds, stick kisses on my eyes,

fill my body with sighs. I so want to reach you
but seaweed's wound round the rungs, round
my feet, my hands . . . there's that woman. The sun

has burnt her white legs a frightful scarlet.
Oh she's shrieking: 'Don't let me down, Katie,
I'll go mad! Don't climb up the ladder!'

Stone

Tom

Even in this blurred photograph
the stone angel's face fills me
with such comforting silence. The wing
that's not worn down by time is raised,
pressed against the head as if to protect it,
the pinions carved a thousand years ago
still have such delicacy. Deerhurst –
my favourite Saxon church. I remember it

set in a paradise of hot grainy
cornfields, a few miles from that huge
loop of river at Tewskesbury . . . Of course
I could spend the whole of August visiting
Anglo-Saxon churches now Ella's dismissed me
but wouldn't I be hounded by the knowledge
that all I've done is add to her problems?
And the prospect of travelling the country alone

is bleak as stubble fields below endless
grey sky. Today was an ordeal
from the moment we entered her room

and she sneered: 'At last you've found yourself
another wife,' which was so in character
I shouldn't have stood lost for words,
left it to Katie who explained with tact:
'As I'm an old friend of Tom's I suggested

I came along – he's very worried
he's not found the best way to help you.'
'Too right he's not!' Ella snapped
and her matchstick body bridled in contempt.
'Send me away if I'm barging in,'
Katie's reply, low-key, smiling,
produced: 'Why should I fucking mind
if you stay? – might make a change

from boredom. And it's news to me
that anyone cares a fart about what I want.'
'Tom does.' That shut her up
until I was inept enough to fish out:
'What've you been doing this week?'
and was shot down: 'Nothing – the same
as every sodding week.' Katie was on the ball:
'You sound very angry. What is it you want

from Tom?' 'I want him to stop stuffing
his version of me down my throat,
to see our marriage was always a flop.
I longed for a lovely father – the one I had
hated the sight of me so I jumped
at a kind man who was twelve years older.
I know it's my fault but I saw in no time
it was hopeless, pretended as long

as I could. His Master's Voice always
expecting more, hiding disappointment,
stifles me. Under the rubble something
that's me wants to get out of its box,

speak, fend for itself. The person
I love is Dell in the next room. We share
everything, laugh together loud
as hyenas. She likes the *me* I am now,

hugs and kisses me in bed, says
I'm the only one who understands her fear
of nothingness. With Dell I'm not a shit –
I'm important.' She broke down then,
sobbed piteously, let Katie enfold her.
And I watched, frozen, saw myself
as a block of cracked stone, wondered
why I'd never managed to find her

when one question from Katie had made her
pour herself out. I knew they were waiting
for me to fill the silence, managed to say:
'Ella, please tell me how to help –
visit less, stay away altogether?'
'Like I said, admit our marriage is done for –
and keep out of my path all summer,
give me a chance to manage without you.

After that if you're not in charge I s'pose
I could see you sometimes – just as a friend.'
In spite of my mistakes I was let off,
felt freedom leap inside me high
as a salmon travelling a river. She barged
out of the room, yelling: 'I've done it, Dell!'
The enormous woman appeared, opened
her arms: 'I just knew the fire was in you!'

As we drove away I tried to tell Katie
what a blind and blundering fool I'd been
but, generous as ever, she insisted:
'You've been amazingly loyal to a person
who's a hedgehog of insecurities and angers.'

She didn't add and probably gay, sensed
my need for quiet. When we stopped
at her home I croaked: 'Shall we meet soon?'

'I'd like that,' she said, meaning it,
and I saw her face had an angel's radiance . . .
The Deerhurst angel has a human face
but it's rigid as the stone it's carved in.
Katie with her burning bush of hair
makes me think of movement: a door
flying open, small animals scurrying
into hedgerows, bees nuzzling at clover.

The phone! Ella calling to retract every
single word and order me to visit tomorrow
without that woman in tow? . . . 'Katie!'
'You must have found today stressful –
I just wanted to know how you are.'
'Coming to. Katie, I was thinking,
would you spend a sort of holiday with me –
in August – visiting Anglo-Saxon places?'

Scissors

William

While the she-beest is off gard
take the big silverr sissors
from the box by the sowing mashine
and do her down.
While the she-dragon is away from the den
breething fire on other viktims
forget riting on the computter
pull myself upstairs
and with the scisors cut her down.

66

While the she-monster's barrging round Saynsburys
open her grate big cubord
drag her stinkking dresses
off hangars that jutt like boney shoalders,
slice off butons and call them heds
nik sleeves stab wastes
with the sissor pointes
and bring the she-vampire down.
Rip silly blowses and sloppie nickers
make a heep highe as a bonfire
smuther it with her smelly creems
and laugh as the she-dragon shrincks
like a punktured baloon
bleeds to deth.
Then Dad will grinne from eer to eer
pack my casses in the car.
Katie will wave and promis visits.
We'll drive to THE LADDER
where theyll say you <u>can</u> not you can't
and show me sheepe and cows and burds
in feelds full of wilde flowrs
and how to to clime the hi mountins.

Voice

'. . . as if to bang a great
big drum in my ear
he gloried in planning to attack me –
look it's crystal clear
in this cruel poem!' Millie shivers

like a windcaught leaf
and her eyes are raw lights.
'He raided my room, got his paws

67

on the two glitzy outfits
I made to pep myself up,

dragged them to the floor, slit
sleeves and skirts, smeared
creams, dropped my scissors
halfway up the stairs, cheered
when I tripped on them and ricked

my bloody ankle. I bet
he hoped I'd tumble and break
my neck. That's the thanks I get
for being his slave – to wake
and find he hates the sight of me.'

'No no!' Katie clasps her arm
as volcanic sobs break.
'He's frustrated, wants to make
his own decisions.' 'I've given him
everything . . . can't cope any more.'

Millie's body quakes. As she tries
to soothe, encourage, Katie hears
Louis Armstrong emerging
from William's room, a sheer
roll of sunflower-golden sound,

knows she must speak now.
'You see he needs things –'
she twists a strand of hair –
'a chance to spread his wings,
skills I can't teach one-to-one –

and I'm away all August.' Millie
jerks like a startled sheep.
'The point is, studying for exams
is just not enough. He'll leap
forward if he learns to mix

with more people. Forgive me,
I phoned The Ladder, spent
some time talking to the manager.
I was impressed when he went
into detail about their vision,

their interest in live wires
like William. I explained his needs –
his speech. They're a real goldmine
of ideas and resources and he agreed
they'd assess him for a communicator.'

'A what?' 'A computer to carry
about with him which would relay
the words he keyed in,
whatever he wanted to say –
act as his voice. You can cue it

to finish sentences.' Millie nods:
'That would thrill him. You've found
the answer, been our angel
once again,' but she sounds
resigned, her voice quite colourless.

'You've been giving out for years,
really deserve some space
for yourself. That long skirt
you made me with panels of lace –
friends think it looks fantastic.

One of them's asking if you
would make her a dress to wear
at her daughter's wedding, wants
to pay you – that's only fair.'
'You're joking!' Millie's cheeks

grow red as ripe discovery
apples and Katie feels

a spurt of anger that life
has so crushed her self-belief
this woman can't relax into smile.

Touch

Katie

A bat's skimming the air – its cries
skinny somehow in the huge night . . .
it's gone. Nothing but field on field
of silence untouched by the traffic rush –
all that grass, its milky sweetness
rising, seeping through the curtains

into these old beams, the bowl of lavender
on the chest, our bedclothes, our bodies,
the even rhythm of Tom's breath
as he sleeps which is somehow part
of the stillness. The same stillness
in Deerhurst Church this afternoon

as we stepped into the calm of tall
uncluttered walls and a sudden cool
that washed off the day's sticky heat.
Tom's public manner melted and taking
my hand he said: 'Look at this perfect
Anglo-Saxon window.' Then he led me

down the nave to a stone angel
carved on an arch which was once
part of the apse. As we stood speechless
beneath thoughtful human eyes
and a thick crown of hair his excitement
for the past became mine. How far

we've come since our first evening
in that Tudor hotel in Suffolk.
He kept so carefully to history
and questions about Alice and Clara,
kept throwing in jokey comments
which added prickles to the tension –

his wanting, his unreadiness to touch me.
Four days later after stuffing ourselves
on Northumbrian churches and Bede
we turned south and booked for the night
at an inn that was all net and candlewick.
After supper as we drank tea in my room

he let out without warning: 'It's a relief
to be free of Ella but it only happened
because you,' and he stopped my reply
by placing his hand on my mouth, forgot
to hold himself back, kissed my neck,
lips . . . within moments we were both weeping

as if newfound joy couldn't be separate
from years of unhappiness. 'Your beautiful
auburn hair,' he whispered, buried
his face in it. 'A cheat,' I muttered,
'I'm a faded flower, have to colour it,'
and suddenly we were both laughing. Later

we undressed each other, lay wordless
for hours, bathed in the soothe of touching
I think I'd been waiting for all my life.
The next night, each too anxious
to please, we made love. It was easier
to talk about my colourless marriage.

Tonight in this cottage both of us
at last unwound. And though he's not said

one word about *love* I felt it
that afternoon I first took William
to the park – the way light flooded
his face the moment he saw me, his concern

that I should extricate myself from Millie,
his idea, which I wouldn't have formulated,
that I was a natural for teaching kids
in creative writing sessions, his help
in winkling out work in a special school.
And yesterday when we found 'The Ladder'

on a tree-covered hill above Llangollen,
he was just as elated as me to see
William was trying to fit in, his speed
with that communicator. I know he'll find
a sense of purpose and I won't forget
the poem gleefully thrust into my hands:

It jumps out of its box,
the quicke monkee pupet
that's my new voice
pickes up my words
brawdcasts them
to the wide wurld.
I can manipewlate it
to hook attenshun or make jokkes
to argew with the loudist persun
or throw queschuns fast as firewerks.
But my secrett voice
with its wilde rainebowe
of angurr feer longing
could be squawshed
eesily as butercups or dayses
so I keep it hydden in my dark . . .

It's as energetic as his fantasies and rants
about his mother but now the words he revels in
communicate the self . . . which is what
Tom and I have been learning to do
since the day we met in the library.
And the closeness of skin to warm skin

as we lie here tucked together
speaks a language beyond words . . .
That Deerhurst angel is still in my head.
Why is it saying to me: 'The stone
is shifted now?' I must be slipping
into the dark and silver fur of sleep.

WORDS

Lifting the flap of this envelope
which could be packed
with complaint or tenderness
I tip from its beige interior
words I kept in paper pockets for years
as handles for the almost-wordless:

the over and over of names:
house cat cup water,
opposites which helped me define:
you and *me*
like and *hate*
up and *down.*

I can see Andreas letting out
excited gobbets of sound
when he puts *man* underneath
a youth drinking beer, *sleep*
by a woman who's nodded off
in a chair. He pummels his mouth,
puzzled he can't make
his voice behave like mine.

And here is Sylvie collapsing
in laughter as she points
at the card that reads: *happy.*
I ask: 'What are you today?'
She picks up *sad*
and the downturn in her face
speaks the pain clawing her arm,
the snatched children she fears
will always be out of reach.

I spread out my scarf and cover up
the inadequate words. Humming,
she strokes its softness, with one finger
follows the outbursts of colour.
'Red!' she offers triumphantly
and I know she means:
sumptuous magenta
pale rose
hectic poppy
the soothe of violet.

PICASSO AT THE DENTIST'S

Beyond the long metal arms
    which change attitudes with an ape's agility
and manipulate the high-pitched noise that's eating into my mouth,

beyond a low sun angled on my face:
    glimpses of a painting I can't fathom
though its strangely arranged shapes fit together with such intensity.

Is it because I'm feeling jittery
    about the tooth which broke last week,
the chunks which crumbled into grit from another this morning

that I read the largest block
    as a molar standing massive
in a desert, the troubling fuddle disfiguring a lower corner as a cavity?

In the foreground I make out
    two pigmy teeth. Newly extracted,
they've split, are lying raw and helpless on their sides with roots trailing.

Later, peering through the haze
    of spray from the drill I see the central block
has turned into a seafront hotel that's likely to slide over jagged cliffs,

hurtle me into toothless catastrophe.
    'Why are you so worried?' asks the dentist.
She flicks fear and the pulled teeth become grey lobsters waving tentacles.

But what is the ripe bed
    ringed with gold in which one crustacean
is anchored? Not a near-ready September plum, a mouth full of tongue,

not even a sea-anemone
    though the alluring redness is pent
with something animal and living I badly want to unravel, can't.

Crazily life fills this small room:
    a tube glugs with joy as it sucks my dribble,
phones keep crying to be lifted up, the streetdoor chimes bossily

and every few seconds
    the conversation running between dentist
and assistant slips seamlessly from Gujarati to English and back again.

While they prepare a pink mould
    to jam into my jaw I raise myself, see
the signature, its easy sprawl across the canvas and it dawns on me

the main block is a woman's head
    bent over her lap. How did I fail to follow
the dark graffitti of her mouth, the fingers tapering from her hand,

her wrist ringed with a cuff's
    gold edge or the way its red sleeve
flows into the cape of clothed body? How did I fail to recognize

those troubled eyes
    which look down so intently
into the dark of that rockpool where the unshelled self flounders?

LEAVING

We're both smiling but the word *weep*
weighs me down as we accelerate, begin
to shed the suburbs. Even our driveway
rivered with cracks, tugs. Groping
for a cast-iron reason to return, I think

of crucial clothing I forgot to pack:
my mock-velvet scarf steeped
in panther dusk, the cotton square
daubed with lime and shocking pink
which flicks away depression. When I beg

you reverse the car but your face crumples
with misgiving. In our road danger's ripening
among the leaf clusters on the prunus trees
and already the abandoned house smells
of shabby animal. The filing cabinet

coughs up marbled notebooks I never dared
to write in, frail envelopes, ravelled string.
The brightness belling in the coat cupboard
reminds me of a hall where a golden birdcage,
empty of bird, stands on a red runner.

Uncertainly I peel an orange, gather books.
Within these walls I've incubated longings,
made rice swell fivefold in the pan, wrestled
with layers of meaning. It might be easier
to leave if I put on my harlequin dress.

But suppose the threat crouched in the wardrobe
jumps out? Better to grab the shawl
on this shelf. It could envelop a baby –
the one that cried, unsatisfied, every time
I fed him. My bundle's ticking. Before it wails

I'll tiptoe down the wobbly stairs.
Our waiting car is a doe spotted with sun.
Nothing's automatic but as you ease beautifully
to first, through all the gears, I wonder:
is this keeping or could it be letting go?

APFELSTRUDEL

for Erwin

Beneath the perfect powdering of snow:
layer on pastry layer fine as flakes from skin,
petals from a rose. They're interleaved

with apple's cinnamonned moistness trickling
like honey from cells and a taste, a texture
never found in English imitations fills your mouth.

Tears well in your eyes as the years collapse:
you're seven and Mutti's at the kitchen table, leaning
over pallid dough, rolling it thinner and thinner.

One morning red flags with black swastikas
hang from every house but yours and you begin
to learn you're different, hear fear, its breathiness

in the questions your family are always whispering.
There's the day your mother, brother and you
kiss goodbye to Vienna, to taut-faced relatives.

A few survived. Your half-Jewish cousin spent
six years of war crouched in a cupboard. At school
in High Wycombe you learnt to be English.

Today, we're tourists eating apfelstrudel in the café
at the Hotel Bristol, sipping java green tea
served with lemon and sticks of crystal sugar.

You talk about Herr Hitler, his words erupting
from the radio, remember a girl, her voice rising
out of the crowd in crazy rapture. You tell me

he stayed once in this hotel, mention the room number.
Like him we're going to the Opera House,
a place no one in your family thought of visiting.

We'll gaze at pillars, mirrors, tiers of chandeliers,
climb to the plush layers, watch Siegfried,
the perfect hero, forging his sword, killing the dragon.

And we'll be beguiled by the music carrying
the forest bird's words, by triumph's glitter.
When the singing ends we'll cross the road,

come again to this café . . . Back in the world
which has changed so much, so little,
we bite through the perfect snow that powders

each slice to layer on pastry layer fine
as flakes from skin, petals from a rose,
taste the sweet, the bitter, the incongruous.

CINNAMON

At the verge of sienna, the red in paintings
on Pompeii's walls, leopard yellow
stalking forests – perhaps it's my favourite colour.
And if I sand toast with cinnamon it becomes
a magic carpet, flies me to afternoons
when mist wiped the mouth of the Clyde
and its great tongues of water, fudged
everything to a dirty white. So I come

to dried eggs in sullen spoonfuls,
to chocolate – its precious squares rationed,
to that flat Sunday my father
offered a treat of *lion and tiger*
and we listened, two small girls trapped
in liberty bodices, to the secret clatter
in the kitchen. When he wheeled in
the dolls' pram and with slow ceremony

delved beneath the waterproof cover
buttoned over its bassinet, put
egg cups in our hands, the moment
was more magical than any pattern
I could shake up in the kaleidoscope.
Nothing since has tasted as sumptuous
as those wild animals ground
to cinnamon powder and drinking chocolate,

gravelled with hundreds and thousands,
jewelled with the shining silver balls
hoarded for the ice rinks of birthday cakes.
It was as if a tinder box
had been struck in our sitting room,
the dull coals in the grate transformed
to caverns and crags in an Arabian story.
Ahead lay a future glittering

as the hope of gold in an underground seam:
elephant and giraffe, camel and kangaroo.
Slowly it trickled out like sand
through an hour glass – our belief
in Daddy's feats, the games and stories
where absolutely anything was possible.
By the time plenty was creeping back
into the post-war shops

I was too much at risk from the smoulder
of his irritability, sudden blazes of rage
to see his deep disappointment with life.
But there were still revelations.
Sometimes he opened the amazing box
of mathematics, demonstrated the properties of air,
water, and his explanation of The Milky Way,
distant galaxies, lit up my universe.

Now as I stir in the sandy grains
that give body to winter casseroles,
colour the pale flesh of poaching pears,
I think how he outwitted austerity
when he abracadabraed cinnamon into
lion and tiger. Back at my desk
I open a page, tussle words
into lines, wait for take off.

FINDING MY FATHER

(The 1901 Census)

The House

I am trying to fit you at four months,
your father, *a draper's traveller on his own account,*
your mother, your brother David who was twelve,
also Samuel Silverman, a tailor,
his wife, their three children and the boarder,
Woolf Chonen, a boot machinist –
I am trying to squeeze all of you into
that small house, 87 Nelson Street
in the parish of St Philip Stepney, London.

Ninety years later among the re-built
and re-numbered buildings I found
a clutch of narrow terraced dwellings
which hadn't been felled by the twentieth century.
Peering into the dim of a bald brown room,
I made out its black range. Everything tallied
with the one up, one down and basement,
the lavatory and pump in the back yard,
which I'd put together from your stories.

Now it's as if you've returned in full voice
to expound inked facts I've never heard before.
I read them over and over, visualize
how cooking, eating, washing, sleeping,
Yiddish, the Shabbas candles, voices, thoughts,
must have scratched along together, elbowed
for pockets of space, jumbled hopelessly.

And I see how easily it could have happened:
a hand jogged when it was reaching
for the steaming kettle, the spout

tipping water over six-year old Judith,
the unbearable red pain, the scald
of voices. Your sister's name, absent
from the form, is written inside me.

Your Stories

How you were banished to the cloakroom
for kicking teacher and, bored among the coats,
swung on the school bell, watched
in astonishment as classroom doors
burst open, children ran home for lunch.
How you were expelled, caught scarlet fever,
weeks later looked so sweet
teacher took you back into the fold.

How you turned yourself into a steam engine
and, wheels revolving, chugged along
unpaved streets every Sunday to extract
pennies of payment for the bed-linens
your widowed mother had sold.

How when you were one from bottom
of the class your mother addressed you
as 'Thirty-nine' till you rose to tenth,
how you exploded her dream of you as a rabbi
by believing in mathematics and science,
won scholarships at the age of fifteen.

These stories, safe from bedbugs, the chill
of the lavvy in the middle of the night,
entranced your little girls who pictured
poverty as a fairy tale not a mangy dog
that sniffs out the hungry, won't be driven off.

Your children's children were grown up
by the time you described coming out of school
on dark afternoons, buying a penny's worth
of broken biscuits, playing marbles in the road
and having to wait outside when the others went in
for tea until your mother trudged home with her box
of wares, how on frosty nights the cold bit
so deep into your legs you could feel it still.

Poverty

In 1960 I could only afford an attic
with a threadbare mat, hopeless furniture
and a skylight in its sloping ceiling
but to me it was heady, reeked of writers
scribbling white-hot words in garrets.

The landlady who over-rouged yellowed cheeks
but couldn't hide a mean mouth, queened it
on the ground floor where indolent rugs,
once animals, lay on thick white carpet
and oriental jars flaunted in front of mirrors.

Her skivvy, good-natured Mary, a pinafore
always tied to her shapelessness, paddled up
five flights with bucket, mop and carpet sweeper.
Needing a lightbulb one grey morning,
I went down to the basement, was greeted

by sickly damp laced with the stench of sweat
and stale frying, by a child with runny eyes
in a torn vest who slunk away to a dark
which sunlight would never finger.
Blankets curtaining off three double beds

drooped from strings and I was shocked
that Mary had to dwell under the feet
of wealth in a squalor I thought belonged
to history or other countries – in Hampstead too
where I'd expected life to be illumined

by poetry and art. That was the closest I came
to poverty. Now copperplate writing slams me
into it: raw-knuckled drudgery, people herded
in rooms yet unable to staunch cold or cover
their nakedness. Out of this I've sprung.

The Old Testament

Why did you never tell us the names
of your parents? Why did we never ask?
Each time I read that your father
was called Abraham, your mother Rebecca
I want to cry. It's as if both of them
have been unburied, offered to me unbroken,
their bodies threaded with blood and breath,
clad in their ages – he forty, she thirty-eight.
It's as if I could shawl them in warmth:
Abraham who had only four years to live,
Rebecca who was to slog on for a quarter of a century.
I can hear you, baby Isaac, squalling in a box
or drawer or whatever your mother used as a cot.
And I feel as if I, second-named Ruth,
am standing in that field of corn, the air grainy
with ripe seedheads, the sun beating its wings
on my back, feel our direct descent
from the Old Testament's patriarchs and sufferers,
that book full of strange stories you told us
beside a coal fire in your dressing-gown

when we were small. There was Noah
who somehow squeezed two of every animal
into an ark and the baby who floated
in a basket among the bulrushes but grew up
to lead his people to safety through a red sea
which parted its waters as if they were cotton sheets.
But my favourite was Joseph whose father loved him
so much he gave him a many-coloured coat
with meadow greens and purple velvets,
whose brothers tore it from his back
and hurled him into a pit, who after
he was rescued from its deep darkness,
after he'd explained the Pharoah's dreams, wept
to see again those brothers who'd come to Egypt
in search of corn. And at last forgave them.
I remember that forgiveness, how its waters
soothed, wish it was possible to take your hand,
say I forgive you your obsessions, angers,
your need to dominate – all your shortcomings,
as I ask forgiveness for mine.

CÓRDOBA

1. The Mesquita

Entering, I have no sense of walls.
Arches unveil space in every direction
and multiply it. The hugeness shrinks
tourist rabbles to insect knots.

Deep in the sacred forest, bearings lost,
I crane to follow the complexities
in the curves growing out of granite,
marble and fluted alabaster trunks,

gasp at the gold audacity of dome,
the jewel-blue laceries at its crux. Walking
aisle after aisle, I could be travelling
through consciousness, its onion layers,

to uncover the source of that insistent
inner voice which no science
has ever mapped, the whisper of soul
technology has no means to record.

2. Out and About

Emerging, minuscule, uplifted, I'm more sure
than ever the divine is inseparable from
pillars, cobblestones, stamens cramming
flower mouths, folded omelettes

carried to café tables, their shells lying
in cavelike kitchens, from gift shops
whose ceramic dishes rise in towers
that hum with bluebirds on sprigs of yellow,

from chanting trios of Marbella football fans,
inseparable from the old oranges which trees
have shed by the town wall, from the twisting
mediaeval street to Maimonides' statue.

3. The Synagogue

is no bigger than a village hall
in an English meadow, has Moorish arches
with stone tracery fine as lace
above the ladies' gallery and a plaque

whose many grey suns throw out
a dazzle of razor beams. The guide
gabbling in indecipherable English
to a Japanese couple who nod sagely

whenever he pauses, must be saying
the building housed the severely sick
after the Jews were expelled, later became
a chapel. As an immense party mumbles out

the quiet crucial to my religion slips into walls
whose twining patterns, Hebrew words
were hidden for centuries. It sanctifies
every survival against the odds.

THE ORANGE TREES OF SEVILLE

I step from a taxi to a scent that hints
tropical heat, to the glass shine
of doors opening to other lives.
And it's real – the perfume piercing
the air is everywhere, its source
the blossom in small white marriages
on trees nested with globes, each
so orange it carries the red tinge
of a huge moon slung low in the sky.

The trees stand in pairs sweetening
avenue, square, passageway.
And at the centre of old courtyards,
whose Moorish arches lead to rooms
silken with darkness, I come upon them
standing in epiphanies of light
as if they never shed rubbery leaves,
ecstatic blossom, as if their oranges
are the perpetual I'm continually trying
to cup in my hands without questioning
whether *always* is a prize I want.

WATERMELON

At the greengrocer's the conversation is in rapid Greek
as it often is but today there's continual pointing
at the door and voices latch on worry as a bunch
of keys is examined. The lock's turned – something
doesn't fit.
    Unlike the two men the watermelons
are relaxed. Enormous, they sit outside the shop
and welcome the sun that's eating into paving stones,
sandals, legs. Their tough skins, with mustard
and tropical green stripes
        cool the traffic,
its impatient rattle. Dry-mouthed, I ask for a portion.
The greengrocer shoulders a fruit, lays it
on the counter, produces a knife that could saw
sides of meat.
    As he lifts the long blade it quicksilvers
the length of my spine and I see Abraham, hand
glinting as it's raised to strike the beloved son
who is lying bound in passive silence.
The moment of splitting
      is emotional. I gaze at each
blush-red half, breathe in the pristine sweetness.
'Shall I give you a small quarter?' asks the greengrocer
as if he knows about the pulled tendon in my shoulder,
the drooping wing of my arm.
      At home I take
the weighty crescent out of its sea-blue bag.
It's a curved boat, a sliver of raspberry moon,
a cliché smile. Bead necklaces are embedded
in the marbled pink that's so bemused with juice
it's at the verge of liquid.

As I taste I suddenly know
God is not a separate being who demands obedience
and belief but the energy of buds breaking into a crown
of leaves, insects laying eggs, humans inventing, flesh
fattening, all seeds sealed within walls.

AUGUST MORNING

Empress of the back door,
flinging it wide to a garden furred
with minute drops. Pulling off sleep,
its stickiness. Tipping raspberries

into a bowl, fingers sweetened
with pink blood. Out to the park
before mist that's crept from the stream,
thins into dream, before heat and light

are a trap. No dressing-gown here,
no cockatoos. Every blade, every
willow and hawthorn leaf is quiet.
The house – even my rucked night –

could be in another continent.
Wet grass creeps into my socks
and I spread my arms to the silky air,
am five again, telling myself to fly.

Already the dangerous egg of sun
is hatching but I want to stay
with this pale luminosity, with pockets
of dark in the brambled copse

where bats are folded all day
and layers decaying underfoot conceal
cocoons. I'm fumbling for sunglasses
when the oak tree at the wood's edge

cuts out the blinding amber disc.
Branches radiate shafts as if
honey-softened light held in the hub
of roots, had flowed up the trunk

and out through every twig, leaf.
Let me keep this tree, its halo
of rays, and even on skyhidden days
see its divinity within myself.

MOTH

Not crazily circling a plump pear
whose bright scorch it can't resist
but resting on a fullblown peony papering
the wall behind my bedside lamp: small
white wings textured like embroidery threads.

That such a creature should enter, spend
the night with me is a privilege. Next morning
it's gone and absence inhabits me until
I spot it on a banister: the glossy silks
of its opened fan, each edge scalloped.

The Internet, which answers everything, brings up
moths in surprising fur hoods, cloaks that dance
with speckles – but not my visitor; so I return
to its spread pages, make out a shape
curvaceous as a mermaid in a shining body suit,

a being with a pin-knob head
and complex existence of which I know
nothing. But the leap of lightness is snuffed
when I find it on a stair, touch and it remains
motionless. Did I stop its life? Entangled

in loops of guilt is a self of seventeen
hunched at a table in the school library
reading a Virginia Woolf essay, drinking in
each intense detail. I try not to re-live
the pain of following a moth's last moments.

When night is a black square in the back door
I'm drawn to its quivering mingle of glass
and light, to pairs of wings that hanker
for the kitchen's luminous strips. And it flutters
through me: this is the closest I'll come to angels.

GRAPES

Even in the night-time larder
when flamboyant tomatoes and arresting
bottle necks give in to vagueness

each grape is an exuberant wink.
I imagine the beguiling capsules pricked,
skins wrinkling as they leak

though they look certain as glass
as if plucked from the cornucopian table
of a seventeenth-century still life.

Beyond the back door the once
prolific pear tree and the metallic strip
of moon are motionless. I could believe

nothing in the world is moving anywhere
but there is no standing still, not even
on these shelves. Tomorrow

the Moroccan bowl with fish swimming
a yellow sea may lose the last of its cargo
of cherries and when I reach out

for the muesli canister I might elbow
the split lentils into background shadow,
changes which remind me of Morandi

shifting emotion from canvas
to canvas as he rearranges those pale
china jars and bowls, of the ebb

and flow between two people in a house,
the alterations in my mood in a single day
and the continual movement below surfaces:

plum flesh ripening, decay
eating outwards from an apple's core.
Even now I can smell the muskiness

at the heart of the clustered grapes,
the same darkness that inhabits
the thicket in the park, hatches

moth wings, hides muddles
of draggled feathers as they disintegrate.
But these purple bubbles are indifferent

to my fear of losing everything. Glimmering
like laughter, they insist on the moment –
tipping it raw into the mouth.

LAMP

for Anne

Outside the window bay, beyond
the faint echoes of diamond panes
and white uprights night has doubled,
beyond a black width thicker
yet more fluid than sinuous cat,
behind curtains pale as moths: a lamp.

Its calm could be the certainty we try
and snatch to silence voices heavy
as paving stones, to stop calamity choking
down the phone, to stamp on catastrophes
that still live in childhood cupboards
and hatreds that hatch countless eggs.

Or is it one of the small confirmations
we amass: shells to hold the sea in our ears,
garments we make believe beautify
our bodies, words we rush to paper as if
such gestures would prevent that second
when we're switched off, lose everything?

Combing out the dark, surely the lamp
is Henry Vaughan's star *confined*
into a tomb? It's a dazzling eye
which night hasn't found the skill to shut,
an insatiable thirst to winkle out,
a yearning to put a stop to lightlessness.

The lamp is that incandescent moment
when we recognise that plus cannot bloom
unless rooted in minus; that the intensity
from the sun would carry little meaning
if night didn't end every day
by rising with huge wings outspread.

ORPHEUS IN THE UNDERGROUND

Impossible not to collide with heat. It rises
from the labyrinth of passages, platforms
and grime-lined tunnels, descends
from the street with the yellowed grainy air,
sticks to underarms, crotches, hair.

The squeal from neverending escalators competes
with his strumming and he longs for the lochs,
their chilling mists, but the darting flecks
of light when giant caterpillars lurch
from the dark to disgorge and gulp bodies

excite him, so does the variousness of people:
a teenager with arrows painted across
her meek face and a string of spikes
on her lumpy chest; a shrunken bloke
who salutes him with age-spotted fingers;

a black woman majestic in an orange robe
who awards him coins from a raffia bag.
As he plays he thinks of climbing moors
and digging for crabs in the rain on the shore
at Tighnabruaich, his mother outshouting the gulls –

Tighnabruaich, lost when he was fifteen . . .
A girl stops. He notices her doe eyes first,
the fall of her acorn hair, her mice toes
peering from open sandals, and his heart
leaps at the poppy embroidered on her shirt.

His fingers on the guitar, his rushing blood,
his breath halt. 'Play more,' she begs
in a Glasgow accent, her sudden smile
so radiant he shivers. He hints at a reel
to disguise his craving. Her pasty cheeks colour.

*

Side by side the pair are talking
and drinking tea brown as peaty soil
in Jix Snacks. She's watched seals
on the rocks at Innellan, this Glasgow lass,
taken the ferry to Bute. She sings a verse

from a Gaelic song unknown to him
and in spite of all the plate clatter,
the whirring coffee machine and the jabber,
it comes to him poignant as a curlew's mew
cutting the air. He holds down tears.

'I used to do gigs with Andy. He played
the bagpipes and a heap of other instruments –
we studied folk music together at college.'
She pokes her empty cup with a spoon
and when the thin plastic snaps in two,

hugs her chest, sighs. 'He got himself hooked
on smack, tricked me into taking it too –
but I'm shot of all that for ever.' Fear
is icy in his stomach as he notes the scars'
faint circles on her skinny arms.

He wants to touch, to lull her hurt away,
imagines them both on bikes emerging
from trees by the strip of Loch Eck,
the waters squirming with luminous eels
as their wheels eat the bracken miles.

*

They've climbed the four uncarpeted flights
to his attic and she's nested in a basket chair
on shabby cushions. Opening a can of beer,
he reddens: 'I'm sorry it's squalid.' 'Don't be daft,
I love it,' she giggles. 'I have to squeeze

into a hole in a basement that must have been
a broom cupboard. It never gets a drop
of daylight and the damp's always worming
out of the walls. I can breathe here.'
At the open skylight they stand on a chair

hand in hand peering at the heavy
chimney pots jutting from tiled slopes,
at lights pricking the indigo sky.
'Would you let me stay the night?' Her eyes
are moons, her voice a bairn's begging

for a sweet. In the bed he gingerly kisses
the hillocks of her breasts, her taut ribs.
She fondles his hardness, feels it ebb,
knows he's overwhelmed. 'Play your guitar,'
she says and sits up naked, crosslegged

to listen. His fingers speak of a burn
babbling at pebbles and glassing sand,
of glossy marigolds, feelings he can't name.
'I don't want you or your music to be a dream,'
she whispers when he knits his body to hers.

★

Every day standing at an escalator's foot
she sings about love many-cupped
as the purple foxglove, of loss bitter
as rowan berries and lives in tatters,
sings lullabies that are gentle as rabbit ears.

Every day his fingers on the strings tell
of waves that white-lick the shingle
as they peter out, green layerings in woods,
skies crimsonned by the slowly dropping sun.
Mouths soften, exhaustion drains

from stressed faces, the beginnings of hope
creep into abject eyes. Every night
in his meagre attic love is their sheet,
their eiderdown. They listen to rain, its pounce
and slither on the skylight's pane, wake

to intense blue on cloudless mornings.
When cold weather bites they slow-cook
casseroles in his mini-cooker. Then his sleep
is disturbed by a pale worm which slides
never-ending sections across the bed

and hisses: 'What do you most desire?'
'To seal all this happiness in a box,' he croaks.
'A sealed box is a coffin.' He wakes
clenched in fear repeating the words
but the rest of the dream has disappeared.

★

Someone she knows gets them a gig at a club.
The playing and singing bind the audience
in a spell and they're booked to come again.
In the underground's rumbling belly that night
a furious red-haired bloke and his mate

clamp knuckles to her shoulders, propel her
to a quiet passageway. Dazed, he follows,
hears: 'You stupid wee bitch, leaving me
for that git!' 'We're finished, Andy, let me go,'
she gabbles, then screams a warning as the mate

slams her lover's head against the tiled wall.
He struggles uselessly like a fish in a net
as she's dragged away, tries to bite
the raised fist aiming for his jaw, slumps.
'Keep your fucking paws off her or you're dead!'

The words clang in his head as he staggers after
his attacker to the platform. Everything spins.
Before he blacks out he sees her on a train
trapped by Andy's heavy frame, her mouth
plugged with a kiss as the syringe jabs.

★

A lump of granite is lodged in his brain,
his jaw's bolted. Inches away he sees
the rise of trousers to blue. Above
is a brown face whose cheek bones
glisten: 'Best get on the last train, man,

beauty sleep's not allowed here.' He's handed
his unmolested guitar, almost cries
as he's hustled into a carriage. Each time it sways
he's thrust against beery mouths, obscene jokes.
How will he find her in this metropolis?

At last he's forcing floundering legs up
the wooden flights to his attic. Dizzy,
he has to rest on the third-floor stairs.
A woman in a crimson dressing gown appears,
asks: 'Who's been mauling your lovely face?'

When she gives him brandy, strokes his wrist,
he catches the whiff of loneliness. In his room
he sinks onto the hopeless bed, dreams
of his mother buttoned in Christmas red,
her voice digging into the throb of pain:

'If you'd stuck to the violin and taken
that orchestra post you'd be doing fine now.
I knew you'd go to pieces in London, squander
your talent.' He grabs at swirls of white
to smother the words, wakens clawing his sheet.

★

He walks streets which smell of indoor heat
and sour drains, describes her to addicts,
pushers. Searching pubs and dives, he learns
nothing. Sometimes while playing he sees
her gliding towards him, her intense eyes

blue as seawater the sun's kissed
but she always melts like a mirage. 'You must
have lost someone too,' mutters a man
whose cheeks hang in grey pouches of skin.
A fifty quid note is dropped in his box.

Shaken, he packs up, passes a skeleton-
thin figure by the platform, looks back
at the face. It has the faint blue of snow –
it's *hers*. He says her name. 'Go away,'
she trembles, 'With you I was alive –

can't you see I'm as good as dead now.'
From nowhere Andy materializes, sneers:
'Thanks to you she's a fucking waste of time.'
'Then let her come with me.' 'And why
should I do that?' Hating Andy's smirk

he feeds the day's takings into the greedy hand.
'If she can make it up the escalator she's yours.
You go first and don't cheat on the stairs
by trying to help her.' A ghost of a smile
on the girl's face but she shows no sign

of understanding even when her arm's pinched
and 'Bugger off!' is yelled in her ear. 'It's O.K,'
he whispers, 'just follow me.' He hears her
tottering behind him, holds down fear
that she'll collapse on the moving treads.

Near the top there's a stumbling sound. She's ill
or it's a trick of Andy's. Swinging round, he finds
her crouched with knees propping up her chin.
As he touches she falls. 'Don't be dead,' he says
over and over to the open blanks of her eyes.

★

Marooned at the end of the platform, he peers
into the tunnel's dark, longs for nothingness
to put an end to groping through the fog
of her absence. Every day he's tried to drag
from his mind the ambulanceman shaking his head,

the big-hipped nurse in the hospital repeating
like a robot: 'Doctors can only cure those
who have really decided it's goodbye
to drugs for good,' and the pursed: 'No way!'
when he begs to spend the night with her body,

wanting to drink in the serenity of her face
now distant as marble. Dimly he remembers
struggling down long loud corridors,
standing blinded by sobs in an alien street,
walking aimlessly day after day, all fight

lost, has no idea where he's dropped off
to sleep. His stomach's empty as a cave
but eating simply to stay alive
seems pointless. Someone's given him soup
once or twice and it was easier to swallow

than argue. He's surprised he's still carrying
his guitar but he'll never play it again,
never go with her to the Firth, the Kyles,
see her thin face transfigured by smile
while they do a gig. He hums a song

he wrote for her but it's drowned by noise
approaching. Slithers illuminate the rails,
a star bursts in his head and he tells
himself it's a signal as people erupt
from the train. When it moves on he listens

to the quiet and as sound gathers again
he braces himelf to join her. A dog whines,
his shoulder's grasped: 'Don't do it, mate!
I've been there too but I swear it passes.'
A man in a woolly hat guides him to a bench,

pushes a beer bottle into his mouth,
then prods his arm: 'Haven't I heard you
strumming on this station – lifting the day?'
An Alsatian jumps up barking. 'He's not daft,'
the woolly hat nods. 'It was him that sensed

you was in danger. Give us a nice tune –
I bet Prince will quieten.' He doesn't know
why he unzips the guitar but as he plays
his fingers slowly unstiffen and the dog
lies down, snout between paws.

*

'His music's cool and ooh, those eyes!'
'His smile's cute!' 'It's something else I fancy!'
The girls badger him about his boots
which don't match and collapse into fits
of laughter at the idea of cutting him

into little bits to chuck down the moving stairs
but he's too wrapped up in her to notice
the silly teasing. Bored with their game,
the three let out a caterwauling stream
of goodbyes, shove each other down steps.

All he can hear is her voice repeating:
'As long as you play your guitar I'll be alive,
I promise.' All he can see is her face
filling the slanted pane last night,
a moon flooding his sad walls with light.

Door

Everything begins at the tall windows
where the white curtain billowing over the door
to the balcony could be a bridal gown.

From the veiled outside I turn to the wall.
Its willow-green reflects the curtain as a cloak
on headless shoulders. The mirror's only interested

in studying the late-nineteenth century furniture
and the floor is ruled by the sun which has dropped
a rectangle that's so intense it's a trap door.

Slipping through, I come upon De Quincey's
The Confessions of an Opium Eater, its worn cover
the same Indian red as the intricate pattern

of the frieze on the walls above. Handwriting
that's paled records the book was awarded
to A. P. Green for history in 1911.

Five years later in August on the mudfields
of the Somme my Uncle Phil was divided
for good from all the books he loved,

his university place abruptly cancelled.
When she heard, his mother threw her apron
over her head. He'd become history himself

like most of his classmates, lines of boys
still bearing the bloom of school –
their lives blown away like dandelion clocks.

Surfacing, I think of names inscribed on wastes
of wall and how any day can be a door
which opens to a new dimension
or a blinding ray that wipes everything.

The Toy Cupboard

was as pale and boring as the biscuits
a morose mouth offered at tea-time instead of cake.
But opening it
was the first step in shedding
the ordinary: our lino flecked with green, the red bars
ruling the fire, porridge grey as our school jotters.
The moment we touched the crammed shelves
they disgorged their treasures:
a spinning top
whose rod we'd plunged and plunged
until it died for ever, the grand piano, so cool
in its alluring black case
and with real keys
on which we faltered: 'Twinkle twinkle little star'
or hammered discords. But however deep
we dug we knew the cupboard wouldn't yield
the doll we dreamed of:
her china face caressed
by waves of hair, her lips forever in smile,
so we made do by adding brick
to dull brick, magicked
a castle, laid a scenic railway with warped tracks
from a once-clockwork train, fenced off a field
for miniature cows who'd lost their painted farm.
Knotted skipping ropes
turned into telephone wires
taut with messages. But just as trucks
were rescuing ill-treated woolly orphans
a voice ripped
the delicate web round our world, rained
words, compelled us to clear up and the ordinary
smacked down its lid until we climbed into bed.
It began then –

my capacity for turning grit to gold,
for slipping into a place where craving, its long
bony body, could be clothed in silk petals.

Multiplying the Moon

No opening in the house is shut
but the heat's a cage I have to bear.
By the back door where I burnt
my soles this afternoon I long for air

cool as a fish's belly to creep out
of Pymmes Brook up the park slope
to my fence, press the milky smell
of midnight blades to my face. Not

a ruffle, not even the owl
calling like an obsessive ghost
from clots of trees. Upstairs the curtains
are undrawn and I watch my self in a mist

of cotton nightdress that hides scars,
uneven troughs, veins which discolour
skin with spidery purple tributaries.
And there are my other selves, stars

for eyes, leaning towards the windows:
the one with drive who hoards hope,
the limp moaner, the sympathetic self
and she whose glinting thoughts leap

from the dark of her riverbed. None
of these can lower the temperature,
slow or speed up time, shrink hatreds
fostered for centuries, feed rain

to thirsty fields, muzzle the snout
of danger or make safe the small
creature always crouched at my core.
. Powerless then, have I no power at all?

Pushing a pane to its limit, I catch
the moon. Across the window bay
a second jumps whitely into
the blue of night. In the glass I hatch

another and another, bat them from frame
to frame, create a skyful of moons,
ring myself with silver clarity. Cool
begins to whisker the rim of the room.

Beyond

Why resist this small beckoning gate
with warped bluebell-blue struts? Dither
begins. Beyond is a drop – a few steps
and I could slide on taut marram grass
to a ledge's rim where, shocked by screeching
from wings above, water gorging on boulders
below, I'd lose my grip, tumble from
the tenuous perch into nothingness. Safer
to stay in this field, fumble gravel sparkling
on the path or moist leaves wide as tongues,
as calves' ears. I'll test the fence, remember
a child who was always squeezing between
the barbed wires and tearing her clothing, flesh . . .

My feet decide, walk me through – and here's the sea
that rises in my sleep. It's soft as gentian,
not the fierce indigo of school ink.
Snowy heads are rolling slowly towards
a shore of rock shelves and bladderwrack.
I'll unearth my fishing net, smack at pools
for crabs, unstick whelks to hoard as pets,
summon the steamer with hooting funnels, the salt
picnic sun on that beach beyond Dunoon
where paradise was an hour of sugared sand.
I'll scoot again down flights of steps to hang
over the white rails on the esplanade, run
to the sea as if it was unstinting mother . . .

My brain will rust away if I anchor here
so I haul myself up unstable chalk,
slither on scree, grasp at clumps of thrift.
Remembering I'm loved, I shout at wildnesses
where winter berries burn and birds roost,
where wishing trees pungent as needled firs

are laden with drops of laughter. How easily
the sea opens to the sky, its world of islands
smooth as seals basking in lagoons mottled
with pale apricot, of weightless mountains
humans can't wipe out. The peaks are crested
with white curls. I watch them slowly unwind
into the fleece of sheep I long to stroke.

LOOKING AT LIGHT

for John

The sun is a ball that drops, rises, swings forward, suddenly
becomes a shell cracking and spilling crimson yolk
across quiet blue. I pick out a network of winter-thin trees.

Tyre heaps pinken in a yard, cables dazzle, the steel girders
over the track begin to melt and nothing in the city
is dismal any more for light's touch has transformed

every ash-grey patch, patched roof, every pinched road,
grimeladen bridge. Even the bends in pipes are beautiful
as long-necked birds. Already the sky is paling

and I want to hold each second before the bright colours
all leach out, before the day folds away like a butterfly
into the cold dark and is taken for ever. It cannot be –

but surely it cannot be that when a leaf drops, a life stops, it's as if
it has never been? Surely the mind, its searches and sharings,
joys and compassions, will sift into jumbles of roofs, into roots,

into the smoky wings of downward pigeons from the station's struts
and the passengers who are now crowding towards the exit,
into the irises and lips of selves yet to come into being?